CW01081630

1,000,000 Books

are available to read at

———◆———

www.ForgottenBooks.com

———◆———

Read online
Download PDF
Purchase in print

ISBN 978-0-282-58773-4
PIBN 10858000

This book is a reproduction of an important historical work. Forgotten Books uses
state-of-the-art technology to digitally reconstruct the work, preserving the original format
whilst repairing imperfections present in the aged copy. In rare cases, an imperfection in
the original, such as a blemish or missing page, may be replicated in our edition. We do,
however, repair the vast majority of imperfections successfully; any imperfections that
remain are intentionally left to preserve the state of such historical works.

Forgotten Books is a registered trademark of FB &c Ltd.
Copyright © 2018 FB &c Ltd.
FB &c Ltd, Dalton House, 60 Windsor Avenue, London, SW19 2RR.
Company number 08720141. Registered in England and Wales.

For support please visit www.forgottenbooks.com

1 MONTH OF
FREE
READING

at

www.ForgottenBooks.com

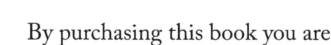

By purchasing this book you are eligible for one month membership to ForgottenBooks.com, giving you unlimited access to our entire collection of over 1,000,000 titles via our web site and mobile apps.

To claim your free month visit: www.forgottenbooks.com/free858000

* Offer is valid for 45 days from date of purchase. Terms and conditions apply.

English
Français
Deutsche
Italiano
Español
Português

www.forgottenbooks.com

Mythology Photography **Fiction**
Fishing Christianity **Art** Cooking
Essays Buddhism Freemasonry
Medicine **Biology** Music **Ancient Egypt** Evolution Carpentry Physics
Dance Geology **Mathematics** Fitness
Shakespeare **Folklore** Yoga Marketing
Confidence Immortality Biographies
Poetry **Psychology** Witchcraft
Electronics Chemistry History **Law**
Accounting **Philosophy** Anthropology
Alchemy Drama Quantum Mechanics
Atheism Sexual Health **Ancient History**
Entrepreneurship Languages Sport
Paleontology Needlework Islam
Metaphysics Investment Archaeology
Parenting Statistics Criminology
Motivational

ALLEN COUNTY PUBLIC LIBRARY

3 1833 01785 6938

GENEALOGY
974.801
L49L
V.6,
NO.10

COOKING UTENSILS AND COOKERY OF OUR GRANDMOTHERS

By MRS. J. MAX HARK
LEBANON, PA.

LARD DIPS, CANDLE STICKS AND LAMPS
or, THE LIGHT OF OTHER DAYS

By MISS MARY L. ROEDEL
LEBANON, PA.

PAPERS READ BEFORE THE

Lebanon County Historical Society

SEPTEMBER 11, 1914

Vol VI   No. 10

Allen County Public Library
900 Webster Street
PO Box 2270
Fort Wayne, IN 46801-2270

Cooking Utensils and Cookery of Our Grandmothers

BY MRS. J. MAX HARK

The most important thing in cookery is the fire. And until a little more than a hundred years ago it was also the most troublesome thing. Now we need but touch a button, and our electric cooker glows. A hundred years ago making the fire was a good deal harder than getting the dinner after one had the fire. For then there were no friction matches even; nothing but sulphur match-sticks, which could be kindled only by the aid of fire otherwise obtained, usually from sparks struck from a flint and steel, and made to fall upon dry powdered punk, or charred wood, and then laboriously fanned into a flame. The sulphur sticks were used only to transfer fire from one place to another.

Let us imagine it, then, transferred to the pile of wood, preferably hickory or birch, for the harder the wood the hotter the fire, which has been laid ready for kindling in the huge open fire-place. For cook-stoves, too, were comparatively rare a hundred years ago, and there are some charming ladies still living here in Lebanon, who remember with reminiscent gusto the delicious pot-pie their mothers used to bake in a pot hanging from a crane in the eight-foot fire-place in the kitchen of their spacious homes that stood, only a few years ago, not more than a block away from where we now are.

The fire-place was furnished with iron or brass fire-dogs and fenders only in the living room and parlor. In the kitchen fire-place hung a swinging crane, from which was suspended a large iron, brass or copper pot or kettle, as might be needed at the time. Sometimes even a flat plate or griddle was thus suspended, on which were baked the buckwheat and other griddle cakes for breakfast. Ordinarily, however, such baking, as also the frying of meats, potatoes, etc., was done either in an iron pan having three legs and a long handle, or on an iron plate which was set on an iron ring having three legs about four to six inches in height. This stood directly over the glowing embers To stir the contents of the pots in which the potatoes, turnips and cabbage, with dumplings, or "knepp." were boiling, a long iron spoon was used. All these iron utensils with the square gridiron were commonly kept hanging against the sides of the fire-place, when not in use. The beautifully polished tea kettle of beaten copper, usually hung from the crane; though it too might be stood on the iron stand before mentioned.

In preserving time the shining round-bottomed kettles, of hammered brass or copper, were brought out and hung over the flames, while the same long handled iron spoon was used for stirring the contents. When. however, it came to boiling apple-butter, there was commonly a stone fire-place built outside, with two heavy forked sticks on either side of it, on which rested a pole of green wood. or sometimes an iron rod, from which the huge iron cauldron was hung. The cider and apples had to be kept stirring all the time, until the apple-butter was done. This was accomplished by having a wooden pole, with a wide paddle fastened to it a foot or two from the one end, resting on the sides of the cauldron, with the paddle inside of it. This was kept moving or stirring in the contents by the person holding the long end of the pole and steadily rotating it with the hands, with the same motion that was used in roasting coffee with the coffee roaster then in use.

The latter, however, was done over the flames in the fire-place. The roaster consisted of a cylinder of sheet-iron about a foot long and eight inches in diameter. An iron rod passed through the cylinder lengthwise and was fastened to it, while at the other end it was fastened into a wooden handle. The coffee beans were put into the roaster through a sliding door at the side of the cylinder. Then the iron rod was rested on a hook at the end of a chain suspended from the crane so that the cylinder was just over the fire. By holding the handle and constantly rotating it, the coffee was kept from burning. Mr. George Krause presented me with the last coffee roaster of the kind he had in stock, and told me then that it was thirty-five years since he had sold the last one. By perforating the cylinder I have converted mine into a very effective corn-popper.

After coffe was roasted it was ground as needed in a little coffee-mill, which one held on one's lap while turning the crank which ground the coffee, which fell into a little drawer at the bottom The "coffee" that was largely used by our ancestors among the Pennsylvania Grmans, however, was not coffee at all, but dried and roasted chickory root, perhaps mixed with rye or wheat and a little "essence"; the same that was almost universally used during the Civil War. Chocolate and cocoa were a rare luxury; and various decoctions of leaves and roots of native herbs were used as "tea." There was however plenty of good fresh milk to drink in those days when the milk-devouring creamery was as yet unknown.

In the country, where one or more cows were kept, butter making was a regular weekly or semi-weekly work. The primitive churn consisted of a high wooden tublike receptacle for the milk, in which a flattened wooden "stomper" was moved up and down, beating and splashing it utnil the butter formed. Later, however, this gave place to the keglike churn, inside of which the wooden splasher was revolved by a crank turned by hand, much to the weariness of the flesh of the child on whom the duty of doing this often fell. When the butter was thick enough, it was taken out and kneaded in a wooden dish until all the milk had been worked out of it, when it was salted and put away in firkins, or moulded into rolls for immediate use. The utensils used, the churn, firkins and wooden dish, were scrubbed immaculately clean, and kept in the "outhouse." or shed, back of the kitchen.

Baking was also done once or twice a week, on regular "bake days." Often the large bake oven was built as an extension to the rear of the fire-place, with the oven door opening into the latter. The floor of it was of brick, or tiles, on which the fire was built of sticks of wood about a yard long

KITCHEN UTENSILS AND CANDLE MOLDS

After the tiles and interior of the oven were hot enough, the loaves of bread dough, and the dozens of pies, were placed on the hot tiles of the hearth by means of a wooden flat shovel with a long handle, all the hot embers and ashes having first been removed with a long iron scraper. The bread dough had been made in a large wooden trough, about two and a half, or three feet long, and a foot or eighteen inches wide; and from there put into round bread baaskets, or wooden dishes, each the size of a loaf, the evening before "bake day." They were usually set to rise in these over night. The trough, bread baskets, shovel and scraper, were likewise kept in the "out kitchen" between bake days; while the earthenware pie plates, or shallow dishes on which the pies were baked, were kept in the kitchen closet, with the other earthenware, milk crocks, vinegar jugs, etc., as also the tin coffe pots, and the decorated tea pot, and other crockery, not to forget the tin candle moulds, and brass or tin candlesticks and fat lamps, and the perforated tin lantern. Probably several leather fire buckets were also kept hanging there.

However experts in the baking of bread and pies, our grandmothers were quite as "handy" in the matter of baking cakes. This might be shown in many ways, and by many cake compounds that by word of mouth have come down to our day. We give here the recipe for an old-time cake for the very peculiar name by which the cake was known, namely, "Schnittels," or by some, "Buwa-Shenkel." This kind of a cake was used at the Moravian Seminary, Bethlehem, Pa., as many years ago as any one can remember. It was made of a rich pie dough, rolled as for pie crust, cut into squares, spread with butter, brown sugar and cinnamon, then folded over to form a triangle, and the edges pressed firmly together, then baked a golden brown.

An old-time ditty that used to go the rounds was this:

> "Wer will gute Kuche bache
> Der muss hawve sieve Sache:
> Butter un' Schmalz,
> Zucher un' Salz,
> Milch un' Mehl,
> Un' Saffrich macht
> Die Kuche gehl."

These were the essentials of the old-time "Leb-kuche."
"Leb" is a contraction of Lieb, love, therefore Love-cake.
This cake was about two inches in thickness, spread out on
tin platters for the bake-oven and when baked came out light
in weight, with a glossy surface on top and a pronounced
saffron color inside. The "Leb-kuche" was in its day a most
popular cake, especially at Fairs and other public gatherings,
and whilst yet fresh was so delicious! Some of our older
people may yet remember "Mother" Graeff and her little
candy store on Cumberland Street, west of Ninth. She always carried a stock of Leb-kuche with her candies.

In the "out kitchen" could also be seen the sour-kraut cut-
ter, for cutting the cabbage, and the "stenner," or "kivvel"
as the Pennsylvania-German called the high, narrow wooden
tub into which the cut cabbage was tightly packed with a
heavy "stomper," and salted, and then put away and weight-
ed down with a big stone, until thoroughly ripened and fit for
use. Similarly the meat axe and butcher knives, not to mention the bristle scraper, sausage-meat cutting block, and later
the sausage filler, or press with a tin spout, and other utensils
used on the annual hog butchering days, were stored away.

Table furniture consisted of china plates, sometimes decorated, oftener plain, a decorated china sugar bowl, a similar
gravy bowl, platters, tureens, and steel knives and forks. As
it was not good form to eat with the fork, this instrument
had only two tines, with a wooden or horn handle. The
knives, being used for conveying the food to the mouth as
well as for cutting it, had wide steel blades, which were sometimes curved and broad at the ends the better to carry their
load. The pewter spoons were very much like our silver
spoons of the present day; though I have a hand-made one
of an earlier age, which has a round bowl and a straight, per-
fectly plain, rather long handle.

From what has been said it will be seen that the kitchen
utensils of our ancestors were quite as numerous as those
of the present, and yet they covered only the necessities of
cooking, while our's minister more to the conveniences and
luxuries. Whether we, with all our improved facilities, have

improved on the actual quality of our cooking or not, is perhaps an open question. Probably our grandmothers would thrive on and enjoy the productions of the modern cuisine as little as we could enjoy those of their labors in the primitive though efficient kitchen of a few generations ago.

Lard Dips, Candle Sticks and Lamps
or the Light of Other Days

BY MISS MARY L. ROEDEL

The origin of artificial lighting is shrouded in the same mystery which surrounds the origin of fire. With the first evening fire came the knowledge that it illumined the darkness within a certain radius. It requires no stretch of the imagination to believe that the next time a belated hunter was heard returning some one snatched a brand from the fire to see if he could carry the light farther into the forest. This being proved the torch was an established fact. What length of time passed between the discovery of the torch and that of a lamp or candle we do not know. Whether the oil lamp or the tallow dip was first used depends upon the nation first attaining that stage of civilization.

Where the olive tree flourished oil was probably used before tallow, but the dip or deep saucer with a dent or small lip; for a wick, formed the first advance. Some of these held but a tablespoonfull of oil and shed a feeble, smoking light. Sheeps tallow and lard were used in Egypt and Asia Minor by the common people. The wealthier class used olive oil and soon had more elaborate lamps. The general shape was that of an egg shell cut in half lengthwise, a handle at the large end, and a lip at the small one. More elaborate lamps were covered, and had a hole in the center for filling and at the end for the wick.

The mounds of Asia Minor and tombs of Egypt reveal the fact that both lamps and candles were in use before the days of Abraham.

The candles of these eastern people were low and placed in the same kind of a vessel as held the oil. Candlesticks not necessarily imply our idea of a candle as is evident by the golden candlestick on the alter of the tabernacle and the lamp which hung before the Holy of Holies altho both used oil from the same vessel. The difference seems to have been that a lamp hung from the ceiling or a bracket in the wall, while a candle stood upon a stand or stick.

The first lamps were made of clay and sun dried. Finer ones were baked, having first been elaborately carved with tracings of flowers or fruits or symbols of the gods. The lamps of each heathen temple were decorated with emblems of that temple. Often the figures were traced in colors before being fired. Lamps were made in brass and bronze, silver and sometimes gold. Candle lamps and their stands were often made of the same material, or the stands were of wood more or less elaborately carved as became the station and purse of the possessor. In Egypt candlesticks as tall as a piano lamp are spoken of, made of metal or wood with many branches; whether oil or candles were used in them is not known.

In colder climes we find the candle as we know it. China claims its invention, also its use in paper lanterns 5000 years befor the time of Christ. Candles of tallow took the place of prepared wood in England in the year 1290. Although lamps and candles came into use so early, they did not banish the torch. It was found early in its use that a torch dipped in pitch, shed a brighter light and burned longer than plain wood.

All nations of whatever time and clime have used the night for banqueting. The torch has shed its radiance and its soot alike over monarch and slave. Rome in her glory used the torch when much light was wanted as did England and France to the beginning of the eighteenth century.

The first lights in our own country were the pine knots, which could be had for the cutting. They burned clear and bright but unless protected dropped pitch from the end. Many a pastor in co'o ial days wrote all of his sermons by the light of the blazing torch or the huge wood fire. Long after candles came into use, the torch was used as a carriage light. Simetimes outriders rode before the coach with torches to light the way and prevent the horses falling into the ruts. A torch bearer went before the sedan chair at night. Torches were fastened to a bracket or ring in the outer wall of inns, and boats carried iron caskets filled with blazing torches when obliged to move at night.

Mr. Higginson wrote in 1630, though New England has no tallow to make candles of, yet by abundance of fish it can afford oil for lamps. But little was used for that purpose, perhaps for lack of lamps or because of the unpleasant odor. As cattle increased every ounce of tallow was saved for candles. When Gov. Winthrop arrived in Massachusetts he promptly wrote to his wife to bring candles with her from England. In 1636 he sent for a large quantity of wicks and tallow. Candles cost four pence apiece which made them costly. Later the silk down of the milk weed was woven into coarse wicks. When these were dipped in saltpeter they burned with a brighter light. Thomas Tussar wrote in England in the sixteenth century, in his "Directions to Housewives":

Wife make thine own candle
Save penny to handle
Provide for thy tallow ere frost cometh in
And make thine own candle ere winter begin.

LAMPS AND LANTERNS

One of the autumn tasks was the making of the winter stock of candles. Conditions in other sections were equally true in our own county. The good wife saved and carefully tried out, deer suet, moose fat and bear's grease for candles. Every particle of grease from pot liquor or fat from meat was used for candle making. This was a hard task as kettles were heavy. Two kettles were hung over the fire and partly filled with tallow. Two long poles were laid from chair to chair. Across these poles the candle rods were placed, each having 6 or 8 wicks hung over it. Small weights were placed at the bottom of each wick to keep it straight when dipped into the tallow. Boards were placed beneath the rods and papers placed over them to prevent the grease spoiling the snowy floor.

Each rod was dipped in turn and returned to its place across the poles to cool and harden before being dipped again. This process must be continued until the candles were the required size. If cooled too quickly the candles cracked. As the tallow cooled the kettle was replaced over the fire to melt and the other kettle taken off. A good maker dipped slowly, but if the room was fairly cool, could make 200 candles in a day. When moulds were used the work was not so hard. A mould held from 2 to 2 dozen candles. These were filled and allowed to stand until cold when the candles were removed and the moulds filled again. In some sections a candlemaker went from house to house making candles. He carried all his tools with him and remained at each home until their supply of candles was made.

During the Civil War many ladies were sent north and made candles to serve until their return. One lady made wax candles 30 feet long, winding them about bottles as the Russians do, and drawing the end through a band around the neck of the bottle. The candle was drawn up each evening until all of it had been used. Wax candles were often made by hand by pressing the heated wax around the wick. All candles, whatever the material were carefully used to the last bit by a little frame of pins and rings called a save all or by a slide in the candlestick that could be raised as the candle burned down. Farmers kept bees as much for the wax as for the honey. A natural and apparently inexhaustible material was found in all the colonies in the bayberry bush, from the berries of which excellent candles were made. Later sperm candles came into use. They are composed of tallow, wax and sperm, are about six inches long and thicker than the old tallow candles. Although shorter they burn brighter and just as long as the old tallow candles, and require no snuffing, which process of cutting off the charred end of the cotton wick quite frequently was a nuisance. An improvement in the material of the wick has quite as much to do with the absence of snuffing, I imagine, as the change of material in the candle. A snuffers and tray always accompanied the candlestick unless as often happened, the candlestick was in the center of a tray when only the snuffers was necessary. Another way of snuffing the burning wick, much in vogue in the absence of snuffers, was to moisten with the tongue the tips of the thumb and the first finger and then top off the burnt wick. This required some expertness in order to escape scorching one's fingers.

The candle moulds were made of tin or pewter, and many candlesticks were of pewter. As the cheaper grades of pewter contained a large amount of lead, our patriotic ancestors melted all they could spare to make bullets during the Revolutionary War. This accounts for so few pewter articles being found today. Brass and silver candlesticks were used as well as those of pressed cut glass. There is something about the candlestick at once homelike and decorative, which appeals not only to the collector of antiques but to the woman who does not know pewter from nickle nor old brass from clever present day counterfeits. For purely decorative purposes the copies are quite as good as the originals and better suited to the purses of most of us. If we accept copies of old furniture why not of old candlesticks if the pattern and workmanship are good. The modern solid silver, if a good make and weight are selected, will serve to pass on to posterity equally as well as those of by gone centuries. Silver plate candlesticks are made in the same patterns as the solid ones, and every one knows the wearing qualities of good plate.

Sheffield ware is unique and belongs to a period of its own.

There is no new Sheffield ware, it is a lost art. If you happen to possess a piece of Sheffield silver, preserve it tenderly; do not have it replated for that destroys its value. Old glass candlesticks are rare, and rarer still are those with glass pendants, perhaps because of the attraction these sparkling, jingling lustres had for the children. Occasionally in the old days brass and silver candlesticks with glass pendants were seen. These were usually in candlelabra sets, the center one holding 3 candles the others one, or in pairs holding 1, 2, 3 or 5 candles each. Candlesticks of bronze or china were found in many odd designs and can sometimes be found in old homes today. The chandelier was a wooden or brass hoop with candles fastened to it, or sometimes two pieces of metal placed at right angles having one or two candles on each arm. Candlesticks were often made of wood to match the bedroom set and used in pairs on my lady's dressing table.

Much of the family life centered about the candle. In summer God made the days long for the ripening and harvesting of the crops. In winter the housewife and her helpers needed them just as long to spin the flax and wool and weave it into cloth for her household so the days must be lengthened by the candle. The stockings could be knit by the light of the huge wood fire, but for finer work the candle must be used. Many of the bead bags and much of the fine lace and needlework handed down to us from our grandmothers and great grandmothers was done by the light of the precious candle.

Although there was plenty of whale and fish oil to burn, lamps were not used in America for many years. Betty lamps were among the earliest and may still be found in use in country homes. I well remember a Betty lamp suspended above the stove in the kitchen of one of our well to do farmers. It was filled with tallow or lard. (They called it a lard lamp or dip) the wick was placed in the nose. Among the very poor the lard dip was a saucer or perhaps a small gourd, anything that would hold a spoonful of lard and a rag for a wick. The light was as poor as the vessel that held it. Pewter was a favorite material for lamps, especially for those of whale oil, which was used as early as 1712.

The tall, solid brass hand-wrought candle stick, number 9 from left to right, exhibited by H. H. Ulrich, Lebanon, Pa., was secured at the famous Carlyle House at Alexandria, Virginia, and is claimed to have been one of the lights used in illuminating this historic mansion in colonial days and during the time General Braddook occupied this Virginia homestead as his headquarters during the French and Indian War. Here in 1755 the details of General Braddock's expedition against Fort Duquesne were arranged by that unfortunate officer together with the Governors of New York, Pennsylvania, Maryland, Virginia and North Carolina, and with the exception of one or two changes that time has rendered necessary, the room in which the conference took place remains as it was then. This old, well preserved mansion was erected in 1752, and is left as a link in the chain that binds the present to the past.

They were poor things at best, smoky and ill smelling and candles were used at all elegant entertainments, even if they did drip from chandelier and sconce and ruin the dresses and coats of the belles and beaus. The lard lamps used at the close of the eighteenth century may have been copied after the earlier whale oil lamps and were quite distinct from the lard oil lamps used a half century later. The one in the illustration with snuffers and oil can beside it was made in Schaefferstown in 1799.

Many of the old pewter and glass lamps had two wicks. The bulls eye lamp had two wicks and a bulls eye of clear glass on either side the wicks and gave a brilliant light for the century of its use. Then came the lard oil lamps. These were usually of glass and glass chimneys were used on them. The lard was melted and poured into the lamp, the burner screwed on and the lamp lighted. The heat from the light kept the lard in a liquid state. When lamps came into general use again 20 or 30 years ago, many of these lard oil lamps were fitted with new burners and used and the old glass lamps in use today are the original lard oil lamps. Last winter at the sale of the late Augustus Forry a lard oil lamp sold for $100.00.

The fluid lamp, in which a mixture of camphene (oil of terpentine) and alcohol was burned, was used for a short period. These lamps had a metal or glass cap to cover the wicks when not in use and prevent evaporation. Some of them were filled with cotton to prevent spilling the inflammable fluid should they be tipped by a careless hand. The first coal oil was used in these same lamps and kept the name of fluid.

Few specimens of the economy lamp remain but it deserves mention. During the six working days of the week it seemed an ordinary brass candlestick, but upon Sabbath the candle and its socket were removed, this revealed a larger socket in which a bowl containing oil was placed. The finer light was used only on Sunday and marked the difference between that day and the remainder of the week.

Another light has come down to us from colonial days which like the first lights, was sometimes a candle and sometimes a lamp. I mean the old lantern. In the childhood days of our parents and grandparents and farther down the line, the lantern held asociations as dear as the old oaken bucket, although I do not find it celebrated in poetry. At early candle light the lantern was lighted and placed near the large fire place. From there it was taken by the farmer as he went about his chores night and morning. Its welcome light greeted the traveler who arrived after dark. It lighted the way to the cellar for the toothsome apple to be set before the fire or hung by a string from the mantle board until the skins began to crack and show the juicy puffiness within, when they were taken by each in turn and eaten with a relish. There was often great rivalry to see whose apple would be the first to crack. Equally dear was the trip to the shed loft for nuts to be cracked by the light of the blazing fire. The first lanterns had horn sides and served only to make darkness visible. Everyone who went out after dark carried a lantern and as the young people started home from quilting parties, husking bees, apple parings or frolics. the dancing lights were a merry sight. When a number of pinched or punched tin lanterns were carried, the lights from the many punctures resembled a lot of fire flies on a summer evening. Happy was the girl who received a gift of a pinched lantern in a new or odd design. Candles were always burned in these

The old town watchman and his lantern have passed away, but those who knew him always speak of him with a smile. The watcher at night looked for the light of his lantern on the ceiling and listened to hear how the hours were passing and the state of the weather. If he called the hour and "all is well," they knew the night was clear. "Past four o'clock and a cloudy morning." told its own tale as did five o'clock. and a sissling and kissling. which meant sleet. The watchman was the town a'arm o'clock. Those wishing to take the stage asked him to call them and with his call of three o'clock came his ponderous knock upon the door. When there were no men in the family, he often returned with his lantern to take the ladies to the stage, which in Lebanon left for Reading at 4 a. m.

The introduction of gas came in 1848. Pennsylvania was slow to introduce gas. There is something amusing in the story of the fight against the introduction of gas, when it was first tried. There were serious persons who actually were fearful that the poisonous vapor would in some unaccountable manner, which, of course, they could not describe, destroy the population and perhaps cause explosions of the most awful character. The original gas light was the open flame burner, but in time a new thought was taken up, that of making incandescent mantle lamps. These are considered the best gas lamps today. The electric light is already trying to displace the gas lamp. Now although gas and electricity have come into general use, the old lamps and candles linger as did the torch in its time. Candles are used on all festive occasions and I doubt if any one will ever cling to gas or electric light with the love we all have for the old candle and its stick